WE ARE THE PLANETS

by Isla Grace Green

First published in the UK in 2020 by Stour Valley Publishing

A CIP Catalogue Record of this book is available from the British Library

ISBN: 978-1-913450-11-3 (PB))

Printed & Bound by Mixam UK Ltd, Watford, UK for:

Stour Valley Publishing
3 Tiberius Close
Haverhill
CB9 0NP
www.stourvalleypublishing.co.uk

WE ARE THE PLANETS

by Isla Grace Green

MERCURY

Hello, my name is **MERCURY**.

I am the closest planet to the **SUN**.

I am also the smallest planet.

You would not be able to live on me
because I am far **TOO HOT**.

I am not as hot as my next door
neighbour, **VENUS**.

I am planet **NUMBER ONE**.

VENUS

Hi! My name is **VENUS**.

I am the **HOTTEST** planet.

You can't visit me because I am too hot and I am covered with **LAVA**.

I am all **ALONE** and I don't have any moons.

I am planet **NUMBER TWO**.

EARTH

Hello my friends!

You all know me, I am **EARTH**.

I am (**PROBABLY**) the only planet with **LIFE**.

I am in a special place called the **GOLDILOCKS ZONE**.

This means I am the perfect distance from the **SUN**.

I am not too hot, and not too cold.

I am **juuuuussst** right!

I am planet **NUMBER THREE**.

MARS

Hi neighbours, it's nice to meet you.

I am **MARS**.

SCIENTISTS sent robots called **ROVERS** to me and they found **ICE**.

This is **EXCITING** because it means I could have had **LIFE** on me.

I am planet **NUMBER FOUR**.

JUPITER

Hello!

I am **JUPITER** and I am the **BIGGEST** planet.

I am **SO** big that all of the other planets could fit **INSIDE** me.

I am a **GAS GIANT** so you can't visit me because I have no ground to walk on.

I am planet **NUMBER FIVE**.

SATURN

Hello!

I am **SATURN**.

I have **RINGS** around me made of **DUST** and **ICE**.

Like **JUPITER**, I am a **GAS GIANT** so you cannot visit me.

I am the second biggest planet and I have **EIGHTY TWO** moons!

I am planet **NUMBER SIX**.

URANUS

Hi! It's nice to meet you.

I am **URANUS**.

I am on my **SIDE** because a long time ago something **REALLY BIG** knocked me over.

It is **TOO COLD** for anyone to visit me because I am an **ICE GIANT**.

I have **RINGS**, but not as many as **SATURN**.

I am planet **NUMBER SEVEN**.

NEPTUNE

BRRrrr!!! It's cold over here.

I am **NEPTUNE**.

I am the planet **FARTHEST** from the **SUN**.

I am so far away that it would take **TWELVE YEARS** to get to me in a **SPACECRAFT**!

You could not stay here. It is far **TOO COLD**.

I am the last planet, and I am **NUMBER EIGHT**.

THE END

About the Author

Isla Grace Green is a 6 year old astronomer who is completely fascinated by **SPACE**

She loves **SPACE** so much that she wanted to help other people, people just like you, to become just as fascinated as she is.

She wrote this little book about the

PLANETS

just for you.